Contents

Any words appearing in the text in bold, **like this**, are explained in the Glossary.

What are head lice?

We say head louse for just one of the insects.

head louse

hair

Head lice are **insects**. They live in people's hair. When they move about and feed, they make your head feel itchy.

4

Bug Books
HEAD LOUSE

Karen Hartley, Chris Macro
and Philip Taylor

Heinemann
LIBRARY

www.heinemann.co.uk
Visit our website to find out more information about Heinemann Library books.

To order:
☎ Phone 44 (0) 1865 888066
🖷 Send a fax to 44 (0) 1865 314091
🖥 Visit the Heinemann Bookshop at www.heinemann.co.uk to browse our catalogue and order online.

First published in Great Britain by Heinemann Library,
Halley Court, Jordan Hill, Oxford OX2 8EJ,
a division of Reed Educational and Professional Publishing Ltd.
Heinemann is a registered trademark of Reed Educational and Professional Publishing Ltd.

OXFORD MELBOURNE AUCKLAND
JOHANNESBURG BLANTYRE GABORONE
IBADAN PORTSMOUTH (NH) USA CHICAGO

Designed by Ron Kamen
Illustrated by Alan Fraser at Pennant Illustration
Originated by Ambassador Litho ltd
Printed by South China Printing in Hong Kong/China

ISBN 0 431 01823 5 (hardback)   ISBN 0 431 01828 6 (paperback)
05 04 03 02 01   05 04 03 02 01
10 9 8 7 6 5 4 3 2 1   10 9 8 7 6 5 4 3 2 1

British Library Cataloguing in Publication Data

Hartley, Karen
    Head louse. – (Bug books) (Take-off!)
    1.Pediculus – Juvenile literature
    I.Title II.Macro, Chris, 1940– III.Taylor. Philip, 1949–
    595.7'56

Acknowledgements
The publishers would like to thank the following for permission to reproduce photographs:
Ardea London: John Mason p.9; Bubbles: Ian West p.17, James Lamb p.28, Jennie Woodcock p.24, p.27; Nature Photographers: Nicholas Phelps Brown p.23, NHPA: GI Bernard p.4, Stephen Dalton p.6, p.25; Oxford Scientific Films: Alastair MacEwen p.15, JAL Cooke p.13, p.21, p.22, London Scientific Films p.11, Science Gallery p.5, Scott Camazine p.12; Premaphotos Wildlife: Ken Preston-Mafham p.14; Science Photo Library: Andrew Syred p.7, Bsip Vem p.20, Dr Chris Hale p.10, Dr P Marazzi p.8, Eye of Science p.26, M. Clarke p.16; Sinclair Stammers p.29; Tony Stone: Caroline Wood p.19, Charles Thatcher p.18.

Cover photograph reproduced with permission of NHPA.

Our thanks to Sue Graves and Hilda Reed for their advice and expertise in the preparation of this book.

Every effort has been made to contact copyright holders of any material reproduced in this book. Any omissions will be rectified in subsequent printings if notice is given to the publishers.

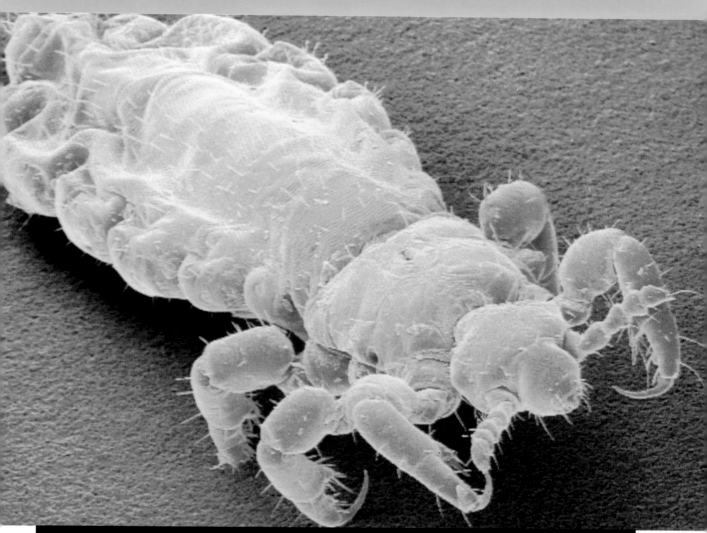

A head louse, which is a parasite because it lives on other animals.

All lice are **parasites**. Different types live on other animals in the fur or hair. Some suck and others bite. The human head louse is a sucking louse.

What do head lice look like?

feelers

A head louse with its soft, flat body and feelers.

body

Head lice do not have wings. They have short **feelers**. The body is soft and flat. Sometimes head lice are white and sometimes they are brown.

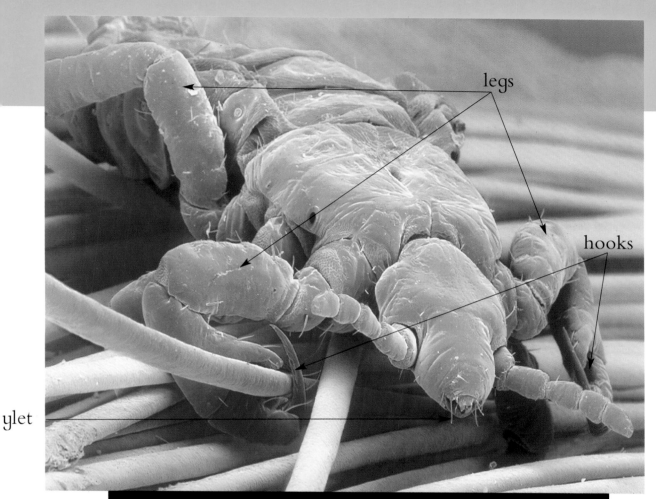

legs

hooks

ylet

A head louse with its short legs and sharp mouthparts.

The sharp mouthparts on head lice are called **stylets**. The lice stick the stylets into people's heads.

Head lice have short legs with hooks that help them to hold on to people's hair. They have sharp mouthparts, too.

How big are head lice?

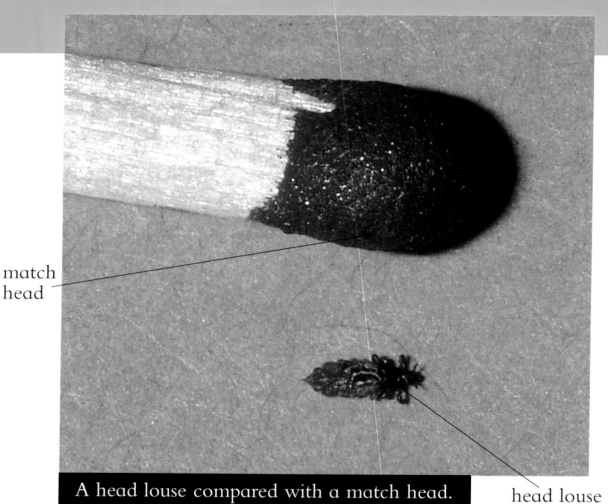

match
head

A head louse compared with a match head.

head louse

Head lice are very tiny. They are about as big as the head of a pin. **Female** head lice are bigger than **male** head lice.

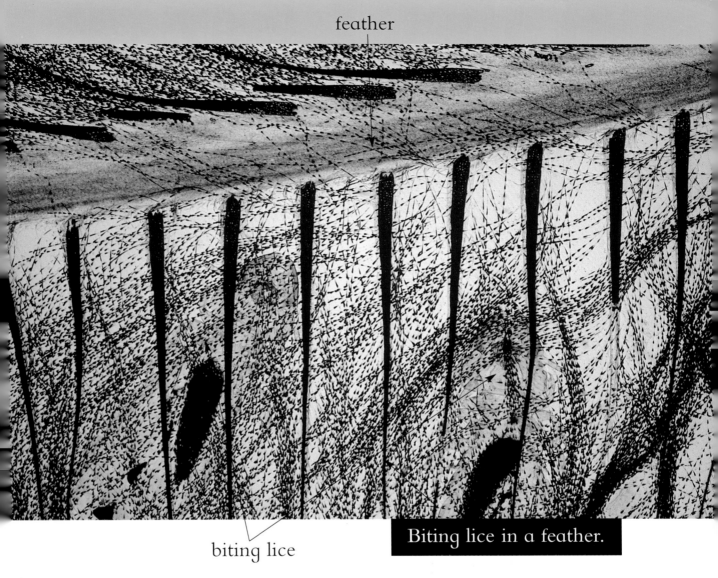

feather

biting lice

Biting lice in a feather.

Some other kinds of lice have bigger heads and smaller bodies than human head lice. Biting lice live on birds and eat bits of skin and feather. They do not suck blood for food.

How are head lice born?

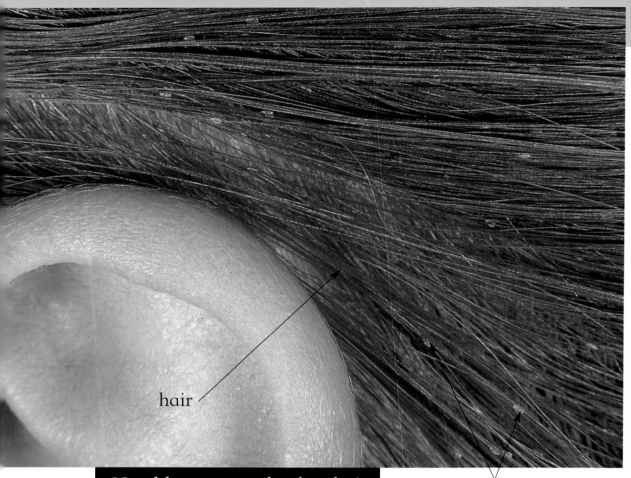

hair

Head louse eggs glued to hair.

eggs

Adult female head lice lay eggs in hair. They glue each egg to a hair. Eggs can be laid one by one or in groups.

Adult female head lice lay about ten eggs a day.

eggshell

The baby head louse ready to hatch from its egg.

baby

When the baby inside the egg is ready to **hatch**, it sucks in air. It blows the air out to helps push itself from the egg.

The empty eggshells are called **nits**.

How do head lice grow?

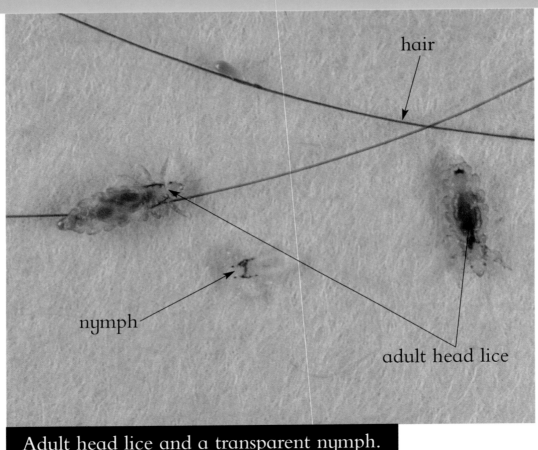

hair

nymph

adult head lice

Adult head lice and a transparent nymph.

Baby head lice are called **nymphs**. The nymphs are **transparent**. They change colour as they grow to match the colour of the hair they live on.

hair

A growing nymph.

When the nymph grows too big for its skin, the skin drops off and there is a new, bigger skin underneath. This is called **moulting**.

A nymph moults three times before it is an **adult**.

What do head lice eat?

head louse

hair

Head lice need to eat blood every five hours.

Human head lice only eat blood that they suck from a person's head. They need to feed every five hours. How many meals will they have in 24 hours?

14

A head louse sucking blood through its stylet.

When the head lice are ready to eat, they
make a hole in the skin with their **stylets**.
Then they suck the blood through these
special tubes.

How do you attack lice?

fine-toothed comb

A boy having his hair combed with a fine-toothed comb.

People feel itchy if they have lice in their hair. Anyone can catch lice, and many people do. When you comb your hair, use a fine-toothed comb and look for the tiny white nits.

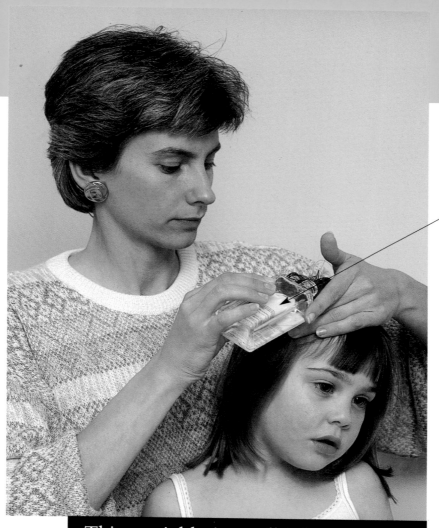

special
lotion

This special lotion will kill all the lice.

Killing the lice is the only way to get rid of them. The lice can be killed using a special lotion.

The chemicals in the lotion kill the lice, so no more eggs are laid.

Where do head lice live?

Anyone can catch head lice.

Most head lice spend all their lives on the head of the same person. Head lice live in the hair of people from all countries.

Head lice live on **adults** as well as children.

Head lice cannot **survive** if they leave the person.

If head lice leave a person's head, they will die.
They need our blood for food and they need
the warmth of our heads.

How do head lice move?

hair

A head louse with its claws gripping tightly onto a hair.

claw

Head lice have three pairs of legs on the front parts of their bodies. They hold onto people's hair using gripping **claws** at the end of their legs.

Head lice do not jump from one person's head to another. They crawl along the hair when one person's head touches another. This is how they move from person to person.

A head louse crawling along a hair.

How long do head lice live?

head louse

A head louse only lives for about three or four weeks.

The whole of the life of a head louse is only three or four weeks long. In this time it can grow big, it can **mate**, and the **female** can lay all her eggs.

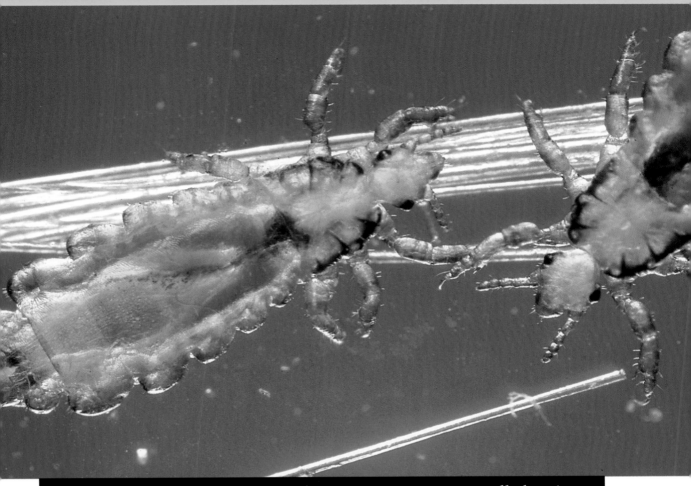

A head louse likes to live at the same temperature all the time.

Living its whole life in someone's hair means that a head louse stays at the same **temperature**.

If a head louse becomes hotter or colder, it will die.

What do head lice do?

When people's heads touch, head lice can crawl from one person to another.

Head lice can tell when another person's head is very close. If people have head lice in their hair, you can sometimes see tiny black **droppings** on their collars.

Some people think that only people with dirty hair have head lice. This is not true. Head lice like clean hair best of all.

Head lice can cling on to clean hair more easily!

Head lice like clean hair.

clean hair

How are head lice special?

Head lice cannot see very well.

eye   head

Although head lice have two eyes, one on each side of the head, they cannot see very well. They can only tell whether it is light or dark.

fine-toothed comb

It is a good idea to comb your hair with a fine-toothed comb.

Head lice squirt a special liquid into our heads so we cannot feel them sucking our blood. This liquid makes the **wound** itch afterwards.

Thinking about head lice

These girls have tied back their long hair.

See if you can answer these questions about head lice.

- Why is it a good idea for people with long hair to tie it back before they go out?

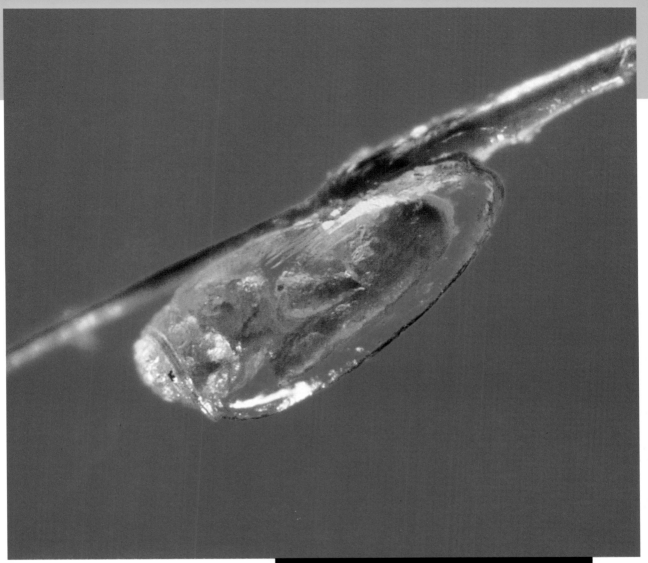

What can you see in this picture?

- Look at this picture. Is it a picture of an egg, a **nymph** or an **adult** head louse?

Bug map

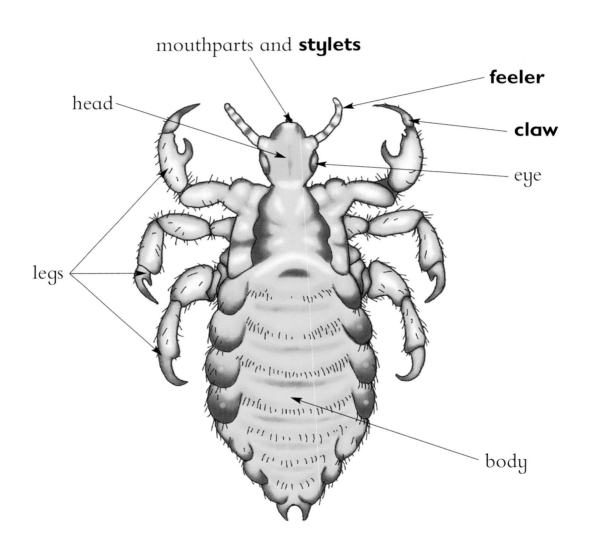

mouthparts and **stylets**

feeler

head

claw

eye

legs

body

Glossary

adult	grown-up
dropping	body waste from an animal
claw	pointed 'foot' used for gripping
feelers	two long thin tubes which stick out from the head of a head louse which help it to know what is around it
female	girl or mother animal
hatch	come out of the egg
insect	a small animal with six legs
male	boy or father animal
mate	when a male and female come together to make babies
moult	when a head louse wriggles out of its old skin
nits	empty eggshells
nymphs	baby head lice
parasite	animal which lives on another animal
stylet	thin, sharp tube which makes a hole in the skin
survive	carry on living
temperature	how hot or cold something is
transparent	you can see through it
wound	broken place on the skin

Index

a b c d e f g h i j k l m n o p q r s t u v w x y z